D0949750

A Year of Teas
at the Elmwood Inn

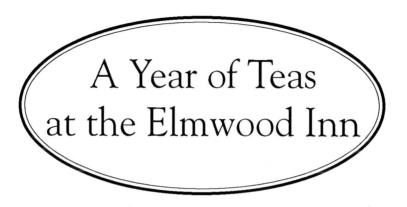

A Year of Teas at the Elmwood Inn

TWELVE MONTHS OF MENUS AND RECIPES

SHELLEY AND BRUCE RICHARDSON

PHOTOGRAPHY BY JOHN GENTRY

Other tea books by Bruce & Shelley Richardson
A TEA FOR ALL SEASONS
THE GREAT TEA ROOMS OF BRITAIN

For information on the complete line of
Elmwood Inn Fine Teas & Gourmet Foods
or to order autographed copies of the Richardsons' books,
call 1-800-765-2139
www.ElmwoodInn.com

Copyright ©1994
Shelley and Bruce Richardson

First Printing 1994
Second Printing 1994
Third Printing 1994
Fourth Printing 1996
Fifth Printing 1997
Sixth Printing 1999

ISBN 1-884532-03-9

Printed in Canada
Friesen Printers

All Rights Reserved.

No part of this work may be reproduced or transmitted in any forms by any means, electrical or mechanical, including photocopying and recording or by any information retrieval system, without advance permission in writing from the authors.

In the Dining Room of the Elmwood Inn.

PREFACE

Our celebration of afternoon tea at Elmwood Inn is an eclectic mixture of English and American customs. We decided that each visit to our tea room should be a new adventure. That is why we create a different menu every month, usually built around a holiday theme. There are no choices to make as you are seated and begin to look over the menu. Course after course is brought to your table on silver trays and antique dishes, dressed with fresh and dried flowers, accompanied by the music of Mozart, Bach, Chopin, or Haydn. Every item is baked fresh in our kitchen each day.

Being musicians, we try to design our tea menu as you would a concert program - something light, something heavy, something old, something new, something serious or classical, and something just for fun! Many of our guests come every month just to see what new goodies we have created. They often bring us suggestions and recipes for foods they have experienced.

The idea of afternoon tea is enjoying a renaissance across the country as fine hotels and inns offer this opportunity to retreat from the hurried pace of the world and enjoy conversation and beautifully-prepared foods in a gracious setting. More than a meal - it is a dramatic scene wherein the guest plays a role equally as important as the food or servers.

The purpose of this book is not just to share recipes with our readers. The broader purpose is to renew a ritual that helps us all feel a bit more civilized. Our most cherished compliment came when visiting newspaper photographer, Jonathan Roberts, reported to his editor that *"the world would be a better place if everyone would have tea at Elmwood Inn once a week"*.

HISTORY OF THE ELMWOOD INN

When Kentuckians think of the village of Perryville, images of blazing cannons and thousands of battling Confederate and Union soldiers generally come to mind. The Army of the Ohio met the Army of the Mississippi there on October 8, 1862, in what would later be known as the bloodiest Civil War battle fought on Kentucky soil. The Greek Revival mansion that would one day be called "Elmwood" was already twenty years old when those opposing armies stumbled upon each other that dry fall day.

John Allen Burton built the eight-room house in 1842 for his wife, Louisiana, and their five children. The home sat on the site where the first Burton clapboard home had burned to the ground. This was the same river bottomland where settlers from Virginia, always on the watch for Indians, had ventured out of the crude stockade, crossed the river, and planted their corn crops before 1800.

John Burton promised Louisiana that their new brick home would be fireproof. The detailed window panels, carved mouldings, and cherry staircase made it one of the finest homes in what was then Mercer County. Elm trees flanked the brick sidewalk that stretched to the banks of the Chaplin River.

The estate grounds covered a city block and included a stable, smoke-house, and the town's only ice-house. Directly across the river stood the Burton's gen-

eral store. A swaying footbridge led from the front yard to the street in front of the town's row of shops that included, among other things, a drugstore and an opera house. This was the center of trade and activity for the western end of the county.

The late Summer and Fall of 1862 brought Confederate armies into Central Kentucky looking for sympathizers. They found few. While the Rebels installed their Confederate governor in Frankfort, Union troops streamed out of Louisville to engage them. The armies collided at Perryville. Over 60,000 troops fought the battle of Perryville. Thousands of casualties were incurred by both armies. The Rebels, realizing they were greatly outnumbered, left in such haste during the night that there was no time to collect their dead and wounded comrades. Townspeople and farmers were left to the grim task of burying the dead and nursing

service as a field hospital. Straw covered the poplar floors to serve as bedding and to absorb the blood. The dining room and library were both used as operating rooms. Detached arms and legs were said to be piled several feet high in the yard underneath the first floor windows. Many Southern boys spent months recuperating in this adopted village far from their families.

The mansion was sold from the Burton family in 1897 to Sarah Griffing and her daughter, Blanche, for the sum of $1500. Sarah and her brother, Professor Thomas Poynter, had been in Perryville for several years teaching at the Ewing Institute, a well-known girls school that still sits on a ridge along the Old Springfield Road. The Poynter family was known for its educators. Another brother was the founder of Science Hill in Shelbyville. The Griffings and Professor Poynter turned the Burton house into a successful boarding school. They named it "Elmwood Academy" after the grove of

A Battle of Perryville reenactment.

the wounded.

The Burton home was pressed into

tall elm trees that then filled the yard.

Sarah Griffing died in 1909, and with the death of Professor Poynter in 1924, Blanche was unable to keep the academy going. She continued to live in the house, renting out rooms to local couples beginning their lives together. Her piano lessons gave her a small income until her death in 1956. (Many of Miss Blanche's former students still visit Elmwood and speak of her with great respect – as if her ghost were still present.) Sadly, with Blanche's death the house changed hands several times and fell into disrepair.

Elmwood was rescued by a group of local preservationists in 1974, placed on the *National Register of Historic Places*, and designated as a *Kentucky Landmark* by the governor. The aging brick mansion was restored with the addition of a new kitchen and second floor banquet room. It then became Elmwood Inn, known for its fine Southern cooking and hospitality. President Ronald Reagan and Colonel Harlan Sanders were just two of the dignitaries who were hosted in the six dining rooms over the years.

The Burton mansion's life as a restaurant ended when it closed in 1989. Without a buyer to keep the business intact, the owners were forced to auction off the contents on a bitterly cold Saturday in January of 1990. Once again, the future of the house was uncertain. One of the area's best-known landmarks lay empty, leaking, and quiet.

In April of that year, I noticed a realtor's "open house" announcement in the newspaper. Bruce and I had eaten at Elmwood with our young son, Benjamin, countless times over the years. It was hard to believe that no one was interested in this aging beauty. We decided to see the old place one more time.

It had been over a year since we had

last been inside the inn. It seemed strange, yet exciting, to walk through the empty rooms with our flashlight and remember times we had been there with friends. There was a musty smell in the air from a leak that had come in the roof. Wallpaper was beginning to peel away from the walls and the paint was faded. The kitchen was a disaster area where stubby pipes and wires protruded from the floor and walls after the equipment and appliances had all been carried off. Plaster had fallen off the wall in one room from outside moisture damage. Yet, the house seemed solid, patient, and in need of someone to once again bring it back to life.

We immediately saw the possibilities of restoring the house for our home with the inclusion of bed and breakfast accommodations and a tea room. Bruce drew up preliminary plans that evening and a local contractor friend was consulted to advise us on the stability of the building. By week's end, a realtor was selected to negotiate the price and a contract was signed.

Workmen began the task of turning the 148-year-old building back into a home on July 15, 1990. Bruce served as the general contractor, hiring local craftsmen who had worked with him before. The renovation proceeded at an intense pace and the Richardson family moved in on September 24 – an incredible ten weeks later! The first overnight guests arrived two weeks later for the annual Battlefield Re-enactment Weekend just as the last painter was going out the back door.

Guests from nearly every state and many foreign countries have found their way to the new Elmwood Inn since that October weekend. Brass bands and civil war re-enactors once again can be found gathered throughout the year on the front lawn of the great house. Local residents and tourists gather in the dining room for formal afternoon tea. Overnight guests enjoy the well-stocked library and the quiet solitude that can only be found in a small town.

The home has a gracious feeling of warmth and hospitality that guests sense upon entering the front door. It is as if the accumulated spirits of 150 years have left their energy there and the house is glad to be alive once again. Surely, Miss Blanche would be pleased to hear beautiful music coming from the parlor piano once more.

Shelley Richardson

TWELVE MONTHS OF

MENUS AND RECIPES

An old Scottish tea with Dundee Cake.

JANUARY AFTERNOON TEA

Dundee Cake
Cheese Straws
Lemon Curd Tarts
Butterscotch Muffins
Cream Cheese and Ham Sandwiches
Scones with Orange Marmalade
Chocolate Raspberry Cake
Seelbach Cookies
Savory Tartlets

Scottish Dundee Cake

Bruce makes the Dundee Cake for our winter teas. His version is moist and rich with hints of marmalade that will remind you of a Scottish tea room.

2	cups all-purpose flour	16	ounces mixed candied fruits
1 1/2	teaspoons baking powder	1	cup golden raisins
3/4	cup butter, room temperature	1/2	cup blanched almonds
3/4	cup sugar	1	egg white, slightly beaten
3	eggs, room temperature	1/4	cup orange juice flavored with brandy
1/2	cup orange marmalade		

Preheat oven to 300 F. Grease a 2-inch deep 8-inch cake pan and line it with waxed paper. Sift together flour and baking powder into a medium size bowl. Cream the butter and sugar in a large bowl until light and fluffy. Add eggs, one at a time, then marmalade. Gently fold in flour mixture. Stir in dried fruits and orange juice, mixing well. Pour into cake pan. Arrange almonds in a circular pattern around the top. Brush with egg white. Bake at 300 F for 2-1/2 hours or until an inserted toothpick comes out clean. Cool in pan for about one hour. Turn onto a wire rack. Serves 12.

Cheese Straws

This recipe was given to us by Betty Sivis, a former Perryville resident, who is now a guide at the historical Waveland State Shrine in Lexington.

8	ounces sharp cheddar cheese, grated	1	teaspoon baking powder
1	stick of butter	1	teaspoon salt
1 1/2	cups of unsifted flour	1/4	teaspoon red pepper

Mix cheese and butter together in a large bowl. Add remaining ingredients and mix well by hand. Place dough in a cookie press. Use the small center star insert to push out 2 inch long straws. Bake on an ungreased cookie sheet at 375 F for 10 to 12 minutes. Makes 7-8 dozen straws.

Butterscotch Muffins

The muffin recipe used at Elmwood Inn is the same each month with only the addition of a new ingredient to make for a variety of flavors and textures.

18	ounces quick oats	3	cups all-purpose flour
1	quart (4 cups) buttermilk	4	teaspoons baking powder
1	pound light brown sugar	1	teaspoon salt
1 1/2	cups (3 sticks) margarine, melted & cooled	1 1/2	teaspoons baking soda
6	eggs, slightly beaten	1 1/2	cups butterscotch chips

Mix together oats and buttermilk in a large bowl. Sprinkle brown sugar on top and let mixture stand for one hour.

Preheat oven to 400 F. Grease mini-muffin tins. Mix melted margarine with eggs and set aside. Sift together flour, baking powder, salt, and soda. Set aside. Combine egg mixture with oat mixture. Add the flour mixture and butterscotch chips. Mix together gently. Spoon the batter into mini-muffin tins and bake 7-10 minutes. Makes 12 dozen mini-muffins. These muffins freeze well.

Elmwood Scones

These rich tasting scones are a favorite at the inn. An English tea would not be complete without them.

2	cups all-purpose flour	1/2	cup currants
2	teaspoons baking powder	1/2	cup buttermilk
1/2	teaspoon salt	1	egg
1/4	teaspoon baking soda	1	tablespoon cream
6	tablespoons unsalted cold butter	1	tablespoon sugar

Preheat the oven to 400 F. Lightly grease a large baking sheet. Combine flour, baking powder, salt, and soda. With a pastry blender, cut in butter, mixing it until the mixture resembles coarse crumbs. Mix in currants.

Whisk buttermilk and egg together, then add to flour mixture. Stir together until a soft ball of dough forms. Turn onto a lightly floured surface and knead gently, turning five or six times.

Roll out dough with a floured rolling pin to about 1/2 inch thickness. Using a heart-shaped cookie cutter, cut scones out and place on the baking sheet. Brush the tops lightly with cream and sprinkle with sugar. Bake 10 to 12 minutes or until light brown. Serve warm with lemon curd, clotted cream, or preserves. Makes one dozen scones.

Cream Cheese and Ham Sandwiches

16	slices whole wheat bread	1	cup baked ham, minced
1/4	cup minced onion	1	8 ounce package cream cheese (softened)
1/4	cup minced celery	2	tablespoons mayonnaise

Remove crusts from the bread and cut out into desired shape. Mix the remaining ingredients together. Spread thinly over each cut-out. Add a small sprig of fresh parsley as garnish. Makes 32 open-faced sandwiches.

Chocolate Raspberry Cake

The flavors of chocolate and raspberries give this exquisite cake a richness that is irresistible.

2 squares unsweetened chocolate	1/2 cup shortening
2 cups sifted cake flour (sift before measuring)	1 cup sour cream
1 1/2 cups sugar	2 eggs
1 teaspoon salt	6 ounces raspberry preserves
1 teaspoon vanilla	1/4 cup hot water
1 teaspoon baking soda	

Preheat oven to 350 F. Grease and flour two 8 x 1 1/2 inch layer cake pans. In a double boiler, melt chocolate and let cool. Into a large bowl, sift flour together with sugar, soda, and salt. Add shortening and sour cream. Beat two minutes, scraping sides of the bowl often. Add eggs, vanilla, chocolate, and 1/4 cup hot water. Beat for two minutes. Pour the batter into prepared pans and bake 30 to 35 minutes. Cool for 10 minutes. Remove from pans and cool thoroughly on wire racks. Place one layer of cake on a cake stand. Spread with 6 ounces of raspberry preserves. Top with other layer. Dust with powdered sugar and decorate with flowers and greenery.

Seelbach Cookies

The grand Seelbach Hotel in Louisville serves these delicious cookies to their guests in the evening. We always look forward to finding them on our bedside table when we stay there.

2 sticks plus 3 tablespoons butter, room temp.	1/2 cup oatmeal
1 cup granulated sugar	1 1/2 cups cake flour
3/4 cup light brown sugar	1 1/2 cups bread flour
3 eggs	16 ounces miniature chocolate chips
1/2 teaspoon lemon juice	2 1/2 cups chopped pecans
1 teaspoon baking soda	1/2 teaspoon cinnamon
1 teaspoon vanilla	

Preheat oven to 350 F. Cream butter. Add granulated and brown sugars. Beat together until fluffy. Add eggs, one at a time. Add vanilla and lemon juice. Stir to blend.

Mix baking soda, cinnamon, oatmeal, and both flours together. Incorporate flour mixture into sugar mixture. Add chocolate chips and pecans. Mix just long enough to distribute the ingredients evenly. Drop large tablespoons of the mixture onto an ungreased cookie sheet. Bake until outside layer is slightly firm and soft, about 10 to 12 minutes.

Orange Marmalade

What's more English than marmalade? You can buy an English brand in most supermarkets but why not be adventurous and make your own.

1 quart orange peel, thinly sliced	1 cup thinly sliced lemons (2)
1 quart orange pulp (tied in cheesecloth)	6 cups water
juice from 6 oranges	4 cups sugar

In a large sauce pot, combine orange peel, orange juice, water, bag of pulp, and lemon. Heat to boiling over high heat. Reduce heat and simmer for 2 hours. The peel should be soft and liquid reduced by half. Remove the pulp. Add sugar, stirring until dissolved. Return to rapid boiling and continue until mixture reaches 220 F on a candy thermometer. Pour hot mixture into sterilized jars. Leave 1/2 inch at the top. Seal and process in a simmering water bath for 5 minutes. Cool and store until ready to serve.

Savory Tartlets

These traditional tartlets are served every month in our dining room. Regular guests look forward to the contrast they bring to the sweeter items on the menu.

Short crust pastry:

2 cups flour	2 tablespoons cold water
pinch of salt	1/2 cup cold butter
1 egg yolk	1 teaspoon lemon juice

Sift flour and salt into a medium size bowl. Cut butter in with a pastry blender until mixture resembles course crumbs. In a small bowl, stir together egg yolk and lemon juice. Pour this into flour mixture and add enough cold water to give dough the consistency needed. Turn dough onto a floured surface and knead lightly. Wrap in wax paper and refrigerate for 30 minutes before using.

Filling:

3/4 cup grated sharp cheddar cheese	oregano & basil (fresh or dried), finely chopped
1/2 cup milk	fresh chopped parsley
1 egg	salt and pepper to taste

Preheat the oven to 350 F. Grease a 2-inch tartlet pan. Roll out the pastry on a floured surface. Cut out 12 rounds with a 2 1/2 inch cookie cutter. Line each cup of the tartlet pan with a pastry round. Sprinkle each with 1 tablespoon of cheese. Whisk together egg, milk, salt, and pepper. Pour into pastry shells and sprinkle with herbs. Bake 35 to 40 minutes or until pastry is golden and filling is set. Serve warm. Serves 12.

Lemon Curd Tarts

Short Crust Pastry:

2 cups all-purpose flour	1 egg yolk
pinch of salt	1 tablespoon lemon juice
1 tablespoon superfine sugar	2 tablespoons cold water
1/2 cup cold butter	

Sift flour, salt, and sugar into a medium bowl. Cut butter in with a pastry blender until mixture resembles course crumbs. In a small bowl, stir together egg yolk and lemon juice. Pour into flour mixture and add water to give dough the consistency needed. Turn out onto a floured surface and knead lightly. Wrap in wax paper and refrigerate for 30 minutes.

Preheat oven to 400 F. Grease small muffin tins or tartlet pans. Roll out pastry dough on a lightly floured surface. Line tins or pans with the pastry dough. Bake until lightly brown. Carefully remove pastry shells from pans and cool completely on a rack.

Filling:

raspberry preserves
lemon curd (recipe found in September section)
1   cup fresh whipped cream

Spread 1/8 teaspoon preserves in the bottom of the shell. Next place a teaspoon of lemon curd. Top with fresh whipped cream. Garnish with a very small mint leaf.

Valentine tea featuring Harlequin Fingers, Shortbread Hearts and Macaroon Cake.

FEBRUARY AFTERNOON TEA

Macaroon Cake
Shortbread Hearts
Chicken Salad Puffs
White Chocolate Mousse
Scones with Strawberry Preserves
Chocolate-Dipped Cherries
Harlequin Fingers
Cherry Muffins
Savory Tartlets

Macaroon Cake

6 eggs, separated	1/2 teaspoon coconut extract
1 cup shortening	1/2 teaspoon white vanilla
1/2 cup unsalted butter	3 cups sifted all-purpose flour
3 cups sugar	1 cup milk
1/2 teaspoon almond extract	2 cups shredded coconut

Separate eggs into two large bowls. Allow egg whites to come to room temperature. Preheat oven to 300 F. Grease and flour a 10-inch tube pan.

Beat egg yolks, at high speed, with shortening and butter until well-blended. Gradually begin adding sugar and beat until mixture appears light and fluffy. Add almond, coconut, and vanilla extracts. Beat in flour at low speed, alternating with the milk. Begin and end with flour. Add coconut and blend well. Beat egg whites until stiff peaks form. Gently fold whites into the batter with a wire whisk until well-blended.

Turn the batter into a prepared pan. Bake 2 hours at 300 F or until a cake tester inserted near the center comes out clean. Cool for 15 minutes in the pan. Remove and cool completely on a wire rack. Serves 18.

Chicken Salad Puffs

1 cup cooked chicken breast, chopped	1/2 teaspoon salt
1/4 cup minced celery	dash of white pepper
1/4 cup minced onion	1 tablespoon fresh lemon juice
1/4 cup chopped almonds	1 package frozen mini pastry puffs
1/4 cup mayonnaise	

Combine all ingredients except pastry puffs. Chill. Meanwhile, prepare the pastry puffs according to directions on the package. Stuff each puff with a tablespoon of chicken salad and garnish with fresh parsley.

21

Shortbread Hearts

2 cups unsalted butter	4 cups all-purpose flour
1 cup granulated sugar	1 cup finely chopped almonds
1 teaspoon almond extract	1 cup powdered sugar
dash of salt	

Preheat oven to 325 F. In a large bowl, beat granulated sugar and butter until fluffy. Add almond extract and a dash of salt. Beat well. Add flour and stir until well-mixed. Stir in the almonds. Roll out on a floured board to 1/4 inch thickness. Cut with any heart-shaped cookie cutter.

Place the cookies on an ungreased cookie sheet. Bake for 15-20 minutes. Cookies should not brown. Cool on a wire rack.

To make the glaze, mix together 1 cup of powdered sugar and just enough warm water to make a spreadable icing. Add a touch of red food coloring to give the mixture a pink tint. Spread the icing in a heart pattern on each cookie.

White Chocolate Mousse

We serve our mousse in antique glass dishes surrounded by fresh and dried flowers. You may want to let this be your accompaniment for the Macaroon Cake.

8 ounces white chocolate	1/2 cup sifted powdered sugar
2 cups heavy whipping cream	

In the top of a double boiler, heat the white chocolate over very low heat until it is completely melted. Cool until it is lukewarm.

Beat whipping cream. Gradually add powdered sugar until peaks begin to form. Fold about 1/4 of whipped cream into chocolate, then add remaining whipped cream. Spoon into individual serving dishes and pour raspberry sauce over each serving. Serves 12-15.

Raspberry Sauce

1 10-ounce package of frozen raspberries, thawed	1 tablespoon cornstarch dissolved in 2 table-
1/2 cup sugar	spoons hot water

Combine the ingredients in a small sauce pan. Cook over medium heat until mixture thickens a little. Remove from heat and cool to room temperature or refrigerate until ready to use.

Chocolate-Dipped Cherries

The only dangerous thing about making these sweet creations is that you are tempted to pop a few in your mouth as you dip them. It's just too tempting!

1 jar maraschino cherries with stems	16 ounces of semi-sweet chocolate chips

Melt chocolate chips in the top of a double boiler. (You may add a small amount of paraffin or shortening to keep the chocolate smooth if you wish.) Dip cherries, one by one, into chocolate. Place on a sheet of waxed paper. Place in small decorative paper cups to serve.

Harlequin Fingers

These traditional sandwiches are very elegant and can be made ahead of time. Cover them with a slightly damp tea towel and store in a sealed plastic container.

1 loaf white bread	1 loaf dark bread
1 8-ounce package of softened cream cheese	1 stick of softened butter

Blend cream cheese and butter together in a medium bowl. Set aside. Remove crusts from bread. Trim, making all the slices the same size. (This works better with frozen bread.)

Spread three slices with filling. Stack these slices like a layer cake, alternating white and dark slices. Top with a fourth slice, filling side down. Press the layers together. Wrap with plastic wrap and refrigerate for one hour. Slice into six finger sandwiches with a bread knife. Makes 54 small sandwiches.

Cherry Muffins

18	ounces quick oats	3	cups all-purpose flour
1	quart (4 cups) buttermilk	4	teaspoons baking powder
1	pound light brown sugar	1	teaspoon salt
1 1/2	cups (3 sticks) margarine, melted & cooled	1 1/2	teaspoons baking soda
6	eggs, slightly beaten	1	12-ounce jar cherry preserves

Mix oats and buttermilk in a large bowl. Sprinkle brown sugar on top and let the mixture stand for one hour.

Preheat the oven to 400 F. Grease mini-muffin tins. Mix melted margarine with eggs and set aside. Sift together flour, baking powder, salt, and soda. Set aside. Combine egg mixture and oat mixtures. Add flour mixture and preserves. Mix together gently.

Spoon mixture into mini-muffin tins and bake at 400 F for 7 to 10 minutes.

A private setting for a tea for two, featuring Irish Tea Cakes and Bread Pudding.

MARCH AFTERNOON TEA

Irish Tea Cakes
Irish Potato Cookies
Pineapple Nut Muffins
Irish Soda Bread Scones
with Clotted Cream
Bread Pudding with Orange Sauce
Chocolate-Dipped Apricots
Curry Tea Sandwiches
Savory Tartlets
Benedictine

Irish Tea Cakes

These beautiful cakes are brought to the table on a green depression glass cake plate.

3   eggs, separated and at room temperature
2/3 cup sifted cake flour
1/2 cup sugar

pinch of cream of tartar
1   teaspoon vanilla
4   tablespoons melted butter, cooled

Preheat oven to 350 F. Grease and flour 12 muffin cups. Beat egg yolks for 1 minute. Gradually add sugar and continue beating for 4 minutes. Beat egg whites until foamy. Add a pinch of cream of tartar. Beat until stiff peaks form. Lightly fold 1/3 of whites into the yolk mixture. Then fold in flour and egg whites by thirds. Add butter, mixing gently until blended thoroughly. Spoon into prepared muffin cups, filling half full. Bake for 15 minutes. Cool in pan for 10 minutes and turn out onto a rack.

Filling
1   cup heavy whipping cream
1/4 cup powdered sugar

1/2 teaspoon vanilla
1/4 cup orange marmalade

Whip cream and sugar until stiff. Add vanilla and marmalade. Use a whisk to blend. To assemble the tea cakes, cut a small circle about an inch deep into the top of each cake. Fill hole with 1 tablespoon of whipped cream mixture. Cut top in half and place each side, centers touching, onto the top covering the cream. Dust with powdered sugar and garnish with a green cherry.

Curry Tea Sandwiches

1   8-ounce package cream cheese, room temp.
1/4 cup orange marmalade
1   teaspoon curry powder
1/2 cup flaked coconut

thinly sliced green onion
chopped roasted peanuts
1   pound white bread, crust removed and
    cut into small circles

Combine cream cheese, orange marmalade, and curry. Spread mixture lightly onto cut-outs. Sprinkle a little coconut, chopped peanuts, and green onion on top of each sandwich. Makes 45 sandwiches.

Irish Soda Bread Scones with Clotted Cream

2 cups all-purpose flour	1/2 cup buttermilk
2 teaspoons baking powder	1 egg
1/2 teaspoon salt	1/2 cup chopped walnuts
1/2 teaspoon baking soda	1/2 cup golden raisins
2 tablespoons light brown sugar, packed	1 tablespoon cream
1/2 teaspoon caraway seed	1 tablespoon sugar
6 tablespoons unsalted butter, chilled	

Preheat oven to 400 F. Lightly grease a large baking sheet. Combine flour, baking powder, salt, baking soda, brown sugar, and caraway seed.

With a pastry blender, cut in butter, until the mixture resembles coarse crumbs. Add raisins and nuts. Whisk buttermilk and egg together, then add to flour mixture. Mix together until a soft ball of dough forms.

Turn onto a lightly floured surface and knead gently, turning five or six times. Roll dough out with a floured rolling pin to 1/2 inch thickness.

Using a round biscuit cutter, cut scones out and place on baking sheet. Lightly brush the tops with cream and sprinkle with sugar. Bake 10 to 12 minutes or until light brown. Serve with clotted cream.

Clotted Cream

2 cups very heavy cream   2 tablespoons powdered sugar

Beat cream and sugar until it almost becomes butter.

Benedictine Tea Sandwiches

Miss Jennie Benedict, a well-known Louisville caterer at the turn of the century, is credited with creating this classic sandwich spread.

12 ounces cream cheese, softened to room temp.	salt to taste
1 small onion, grated	1 pound wheat bread, crust removed
2 medium cucumbers, peeled and seeded	and cut out like diamonds
mayonnaise	

Grate cucumbers and combine with the cream cheese. Blend in onion and salt to taste. Stir in a little mayonnaise just to make the mixture spreadable. Spread the mixture evenly over pieces of bread that have been cut out with a cookie cutter. Garnish with a thin slice of cucumber or parsley. Makes about 45 small open-faced sandwiches.

Chocolate-Dipped Apricots

1 1/2 pounds semisweet chocolate morsels   24 dried apricots
1/4   cup vegetable shortening

Melt chocolate morsels in the top of a double boiler over simmering water. Add shortening to keep chocolate smooth. When melted, turn heat off but keep the mixture over the hot water while dipping.

Dip the apricots halfway into the chocolate. Place on a sheet of wax paper and let stand in a cool place. Refrigerate. Makes 24.

Pineapple Nut Muffins

18	ounces quick oats	3	cups all-purpose flour
1	quart (4 cups) buttermilk	4	teaspoons baking powder
1	pound light brown sugar	1	teaspoon salt
1 1/2	cups (3 sticks) margarine, melted & cooled	1 1/2	teaspoons baking soda
6	eggs, slightly beaten	1	12-ounce jar pineapple preserves
1/2	cup chopped pecans		

Mix together oats and buttermilk in a large bowl. Sprinkle brown sugar on top and let mixture stand for one hour.

Preheat oven to 400 F. Grease small mini-muffin tins. Mix melted margarine with the eggs and set aside. Sift together flour, baking powder, salt, and soda. Set aside. Mix egg mixture with oat mixture. Add flour mixture, pecans, and preserves. Mix together gently. Spoon batter into mini-muffin tins and bake 7-10 minutes. Makes 12 dozen mini-muffins. These muffins freeze well.

Irish Potato Cookies

Who would have thought that such an ordinary snack food could add such a distinctive flavor to a traditional shortbread recipe?

1 pound butter, softened	1 1/4 teaspoon vanilla
1 cup sugar	1 1/2 cups crushed potato chips
3 cups all-purpose flour	powdered sugar

Preheat oven to 325 F. Cream butter and sugar together with a mixer. Add flour and vanilla. Using your hands, blend in crushed potato chips. Place heaping teaspoons of dough on a cookie sheet. Bake for 12 minutes or until a light golden brown. Refrigerate the cookies but do not freeze. Dust with powdered sugar just before serving. Makes 3 dozen cookies.

Bread Pudding with Orange Sauce

An old-fashioned dessert with a new twist. Perfect with tea on a chilly March afternoon.

6 ounces day-old bread with crust	1/2 cup butter, melted
2 cups milk	3 tablespoons vanilla
2 eggs	1 tablespoon melted butter
1 cup sugar	

Preheat oven to 350 F. Place the bread into a large mixing bowl. Add milk and let sit until milk is absorbed. In a separate bowl, beat the eggs. Add sugar, butter, and vanilla. Mix well. Add this mixture to bread and milk.. Coat a rounded 2-quart glass baking dish with 1 tablespoon of melted butter. Pour bread mixture into baking dish. Bake at 350 F for 45 minutes to 1 hour. Pudding should be firm and light golden brown. Spoon into separate dessert dishes and serve with sauce.

Orange sauce

1 cup sugar	dash of salt
2 tablespoons cornstarch	4 tablespoons butter
2 cups boiling orange juice	dash of nutmeg
2 tablespoons lemon juice	

Mix sugar and cornstarch. Add to orange juice, stirring constantly. Boil 5 minutes, stirring occasionally. Remove from heat and add remaining ingredients.

Daffodil Cake with Lemon Sauce.

APRIL AFTERNOON TEA

Daffodil Cake
Coconut Pecan Muffins
Apricot Bavarian Cream
Smoked Turkey Sandwiches
Scones with Devonshire Cream
Red Radish Tea Sandwiches
Shortbread Flowers
Chocolate Truffles
Savory Tartlets

Apricot Bavarian Cream

This exquisitely-colored cream comes from the Williamsburg Inn, Williamsburg, Virginia.

1 package orange- flavored gelatin	1 cup crushed apricots, drained
1/4 cup sugar	1 teaspoon almond extract
1 cup apricot juice	1 cup whipping cream

Dissolve gelatin in 1 cup of hot water. Add sugar and apricot juice. Chill until cold and syrupy. Add apricots and almond extract.

Whip cream until soft peaks form. Fold it into gelatin mixture. Spoon into a large glass dish or individual sherbet glasses. Chill until firm. Serves 8.

Shortbread Flowers

Shortbread dough is great for decorating. The firm texture allows it to be easily cut and painted to resemble all sorts of things - from flowers to hearts.

2 cups unsalted butter, room temperature	4 cups all-purpose flour
1 cup sugar	1 cup finely chopped almonds
1 teaspoon almond extract	

Preheat oven to 325 F. In a large bowl beat butter and sugar until fluffy. Add almond extract and a dash of salt. Beat well. Add flour and stir until well mixed. Stir in almonds.

Roll out on a floured board to 1/4 inch thickness. Cut with a flower-shaped cookie cutter. Place cookies on an ungreased cookie sheet. Bake for 15 to 20 minutes. Cookies should not brown. Cool on a wire rack.

Decorate by piping green and yellow icings around the cookies as an outline.

Daffodil Cake with Lemon Sauce

With daffodils blooming right outside our windows and fresh blossoms on the cake plate, this has to be the most eye-catching cake we serve.

White batter:

1/2 cup sifted cake flour	1/2 teaspoon vanilla
1/2 cup sifted powdered sugar	1/8 teaspoon salt
6 egg whites at room temperature	1/2 cup granulated sugar
1/2 teaspoon cream of tartar	

Sift cake flour and powdered sugar together six times. Beat egg whites until frothy. Add cream of tartar, vanilla, and salt. Beat until soft peaks form. Gradually beat in the granulated sugar. Sift a fourth of the flour mixture at a time over the egg mixture; fold in.

Yellow batter:

3/4 cups sifted cake flour	1 tablespoon cold water
3/4 teaspoon baking powder	1/2 cup granulated sugar
6 egg yolks	powdered sugar
2 1/2 tablespoons lemon juice	

Sift cake flour and baking powder together six times. Beat the egg yolks with lemon juice and water until thick, about 5 minutes. Gradually beat in the granulated sugar. Sift a fourth of the flour mixture at a time over the egg mixture; fold in.

Alternately spoon yellow and white mixtures into an ungreased 9 or 10 inch tube pan. Bake at 375 F for 35 to 40 minutes. Invert and cool. Dust the cake with powdered sugar and serve with lemon sauce.

Lemon Sauce:

1/2 cup granulated sugar	2 tablespoons unsalted butter
1 tablespoon corn starch	1 cup boiling water
1/2 cup fresh lemon juice	few grains salt
1 teaspoon lemon zest	

In a medium saucepan, mix together sugar and corn starch. Gradually add boiling water. Boil five minutes. Remove from heat and add fresh lemon juice, zest, butter, and salt.

Chocolate Truffles

1/3 cup butter	1 1/2 teaspoons vanilla extract
1/2 cup cocoa	1/2 teaspoon almond extract
3 cups powdered sugar	powdered sugar and cocoa for coating
1/3 cup heavy whipping cream	

Melt butter. Stir in cocoa and allow to cool. In a large mixing bowl, combine the cocoa mixture with powdered sugar. Gradually add cream, vanilla, and almond extracts, blending well. Chill until firm. Shape small amounts of the mixture into 1 inch balls. Roll in powdered sugar or a mixture of sugar and cocoa until covered. Chill until firm or freeze up to four weeks. Coat again before serving. Makes 3 1/2 dozen.

Red Radish Tea Sandwiches

1 small bunch red radishes, thinly sliced	1/2 stick unsalted butter, room temperature
1 3-ounce package cream cheese, softened	2 tablespoons fresh chopped parsley
salt and pepper to taste	16 slices white bread
	fresh parsley for garnish

Cut bread into rounds using a small biscuit cutter. Mix cream cheese, butter, parsley, salt, and pepper together. Spread a small amount on each piece of bread. Top with a radish slice and a piece of parsley. Place in a plastic container and cover with a damp paper towel. Refrigerate until ready to serve. Makes 32 sandwiches.

Smoked Turkey Tea Sandwiches

1/4 pound smoked turkey, thinly sliced	16 slices rye bread
1/4 cup mayonnaise	olives, thinly sliced
1 tablespoon dijon mustard	parsley

Remove crusts from bread. Use a diamond-shaped cookie cutter to cut bread . Cut pieces of turkey to match the shape of the bread slices. Mix mayonnaise and mustard together and spread thinly over each piece of bread. Place a piece of turkey on top and garnish with an olive slice and a sprig of parsley. Makes 32 open-faced sandwiches.

Elmwood Devonshire Cream
Our version of this English tea classic is made with a sour cream base. Serve with scones.

1 cup heavy whipping cream	1 1/2 teaspoons white vanilla extract
1/2 cup powdered sugar	1 8-ounce carton sour cream

Beat whipping cream, sugar, and vanilla until stiff. Fold sour cream into this mixture and refrigerate. Serve with warm scones.

Coconut Pecan Muffins

18 ounces quick oats	3 cups all-purpose flour
1 quart (4 cups) buttermilk	4 teaspoons baking powder
1 pound light brown sugar	1 teaspoon salt
1 1/2 cups (3 sticks) margarine, melted & cooled	1 1/2 teaspoons baking soda
6 eggs, slightly beaten	1 cup flaked coconut
1 1/2 cups chopped pecans	

Mix together oats and buttermilk in a large bowl. Sprinkle brown sugar on top and let mixture stand for one hour. Preheat oven to 400 F. Grease mini-muffin tins. Mix melted margarine with eggs and set aside. Sift together flour, baking powder, salt, and soda. Set aside. Mix egg mixture with oat mixture. Add flour mixture, pecans, and coconut. Mix together gently.

Spoon batter into mini-muffin tins and bake 7-10 minutes. Makes 12 dozen mini-muffins. These muffins freeze well.

A tiered serving of White Chocolate Strawberries, Savory Tartlets, Scones, Orange Walnut Muffins, Ham and Orange Tea Sandwiches and Cheese and Carrot Tea Sandwiches.

MAY AFTERNOON TEA

Amaretti Cookies
Raspberry Angel Cake
Scones with Honey Butter
White Chocolate Strawberries
Cheese and Carrot Tea Sandwiches
Ham and Orange Sandwiches
Orange Walnut Muffins
Savory Tartlets

Raspberry Angel Cake

This cake is colorful, light, and delicious. I adapted it from a recipe I found in one of my mother's old cookbooks.

1 baked angel food cake, torn into pieces
2 cups whipping cream
2 tablespoons sugar
1 6-ounce package raspberry gelatin

Dash of salt
2 1/2 cups boiling water
1 10-ounce package frozen raspberries, thawed

Dissolve gelatin and salt in boiling water. Add berries and chill until partially set. Beat whipping cream and sugar until stiff. Whip gelatin until fluffy; fold in whipped cream. Set aside.

Spoon small portion of raspberry mixture into bottom of greased angel food cake pan. Add a layer of cake pieces and repeat layering until pan is full. Cover and refrigerate for 6 hours. Unmold and decorate with fresh raspberries or flowers.

Amaretti Cookies

2 egg whites at room temperature
1 1/2 cups ground almonds
1 cup sifted confectioners sugar
1/4 teaspoon salt

1 teaspoon almond extract
1/2 teaspoon vanilla extract
1/4 teaspoon coconut extract

Preheat oven to 300 F. Lightly grease cookie sheets.

Combine ground almonds with sugar and mix well. Beat egg whites with salt until stiff peaks form. Stir almond mixture into beaten egg whites and add the 3 extracts.

Drop by rounded teaspoons onto the prepared cookie sheet allowing 2 inches between each cookie. Bake 15 to 20 minutes, or until light brown. Allow the cookies to cool for 5 to 10 minutes before removing them from the cookie sheet. Cool completely on a wire rack. Makes 2 1/2 to 3 dozen cookies.

White Chocolate Strawberries

1 pint fresh strawberries
6 ounces white chocolate

1 tablespoon shortening

Wash and pat dry the strawberries. Do not hull.

Over low heat, melt white chocolate in the top of a double boiler and add shortening to make coating easier. Hold each strawberry by the stem and dip 2/3 of the way into chocolate. Set strawberries on a sheet of wax paper and cool. Refrigerate until ready to serve.

Orange Walnut Muffins

18	ounces quick oats	3	cups all-purpose flour
1	quart (4 cups) buttermilk	4	teaspoons baking powder
1	pound light brown sugar	1	teaspoon salt
1 1/2	cups (3 sticks) margarine, melted & cooled	1 1/2	teaspoons baking soda
6	eggs, slightly beaten	1	6-ounce jar orange marmalade
1	cup chopped walnuts		

Mix together oats and buttermilk in a large bowl. Sprinkle brown sugar on top and let mixture stand for one hour.

Preheat oven to 400 F. Grease mini-muffin tins. Mix melted margarine with eggs and set aside. Sift together flour, baking powder, salt, and soda. Set aside . Mix egg mixture with oat mixture. Add flour mixture, walnuts, and marmalade. Mix together gently. Spoon batter into muffin tins and bake 7-10 minutes. Makes 12 dozen mini-muffins. These muffins freeze well.

Cheese and Carrot Tea Sandwiches

1 cup grated carrots
1 cup grated sharp cheddar cheese
5 tablespoons mayonnaise
16 slices whole wheat bread

salt and pepper to taste
thin slices of carrot
fresh parsley

Mix together carrots and cheese, mayonnaise, salt and pepper. Remove crusts from bread and cut out round pieces with a small cutter. Spread slices of bread with the cheese mixture. Garnish with a thin slice of carrot and fresh parsley. Makes 32 open-faced sandwiches.

Honey Butter

1 cup unsalted butter, room temperature
1/4 cup honey

1/4 cup powdered sugar

In a medium bowl, mix the butter, honey, and powdered sugar together until fluffy. Store in refrigerator until ready to serve.

Ham and Orange Tea Sandwiches

16 slices pumpernickel bread
2 cups ground cooked lean ham
1/2 cup finely-chopped celery

6 tablespoons mayonnaise
32 mandarin orange sections
fresh parsley

Combine ham, celery, and mayonnaise in a bowl. Mix well. Remove crusts from each slice of bread and cut into diamond shapes. Spread a layer of ham mixture over each slice of bread and garnish with fresh parsley and orange sections. Makes 32 open-faced sandwiches.

An afternoon June tea with Victorian Poppy Seed Cake.

JUNE AFTERNOON TEA

Lemon Tarts
Strawberry Sorbet
Chocolate Shortbread
Stuffed Cherry Tomatoes
Cucumber Tea Sandwiches
Victorian Poppy Seed Cake
Scones with Peach Butter
English Savory Tartlets
Strawberry Muffins

Lemon Tarts

Tart Shells

2   cups all-purpose flour
pinch of salt
1/2 cup shortening, well chilled

4 to 5 tablespoons cold water
1/2 cup butter, well chilled
mini-muffin tins

Preheat oven to 450 F. Mix together flour and salt. With a pastry blender, cut butter and shortening into flour until mixture resembles coarse meal. Add cold water, a little at a time, until mixture is moist enough to form a ball. Do not overmix. Cover and chill 15 minutes. On a floured surface, roll pastry out with a floured rolling pin. Grease mini-muffin tins. Cut pastry into 3-inch circles and press each circle into a muffin cup. Bake for 8 minutes. Cool completely. Fill with lemon mixture.

Lemon Filling

1/2   cup fresh lemon juice
1 1/2 cups sugar

3/4 cups unsalted butter, melted
4   eggs, beaten

In a large sauce pan, combine lemon juice, sugar, and butter. Stir in eggs. Cook over low heat, stirring constantly, until the mixture thickens. This should take 20 minutes. Cool slightly or refrigerate until ready to serve. Place a tablespoon of the filling into each tart shell. Garnish with a fresh blueberry and tiny mint leaf.

Peach Butter

1   cup unsalted butter, softened
1/2 cup peach preserves

1/4 cup powdered sugar

In a small bowl, mix all ingredients thoroughly. Refrigerate until read to serve. Use a small scoop to make small butter balls. Serve with warm scones.

Chocolate Shortbread

2 cups unsalted butter, room temperature
1 cup sugar
1 teaspoon almond extract

4 cups all-purpose flour
1 cup finely-chopped almonds
2 squares unsweetened chocolate, melted

Preheat oven to 325 F. In a large bowl, beat butter and sugar until fluffy. Add almond extract and a dash of salt. Beat well.

Add flour and stir until well-mixed. Stir in almonds and melted chocolate. Roll out on a floured board to 1/4 inch thickness. Cut out with a teddy bear cookie cutter. Place cookies on an ungreased cookie sheet. Bake for 15-20 minutes. Cool on a wire rack.

Victorian Poppy Seed Cake
with Lime Syrup

We serve this Victorian cake on an antique glass cake stand and garnish it with fresh lavender from our herb garden.

1 cup unsalted butter, room temperature
1 cup sugar
4 egg yolks
1/4 cup poppy seeds
2 cups cake flour
1 teaspoon baking soda

1 cup sour cream
4 egg whites, stiffly beaten
1 teaspoon almond extract
1 teaspoon vanilla extract
1 teaspoon cinnamon

Preheat oven to 350 F. Grease and flour a 10-inch tube pan. Cream butter, sugar, egg yolks, and poppy seeds. Sift together flour and baking soda. Add flour mixture to creamed mixture, alternating with sour cream. Begin and end with flour mixture.

Combine beaten egg whites, almond extract, vanilla extract, and cinnamon. Fold into batter. Pour mixture into a prepared tube pan and bake 50 to 60 minutes or until a cake tester comes out clean. Top immediately with lime syrup. Cool in pan. Serves 15-20.

Lime Syrup

1/2 cup fresh lime juice

1/3 cup superfine sugar

Stir juice and sugar together until sugar is dissolved. Pour over hot cake.

Stuffed Cherry Tomatoes

1 pint cherry tomatoes
3 ounces chevre (goat) cheese, softened
2 teaspoons fresh basil, chopped
1 tablespoon fresh parsley, chopped

1 teaspoon fresh oregano, chopped
1 teaspoon crushed garlic
1 teaspoon white wine worcestershire

Wash and dry tomatoes. Place stem side down, then cut an X across the top, halfway through. Combine cheese, herbs, and worcestershire. Pipe or spoon mixture into cut of tomato. Garnish with fresh parsley. Makes 20 to 30 servings.

Strawberry Sorbet

1 1/2 cups ice cold water
1/4   cup powdered sugar
fresh strawberries

2 10-ounce packages frozen strawberries in syrup,
   thawed
fresh mint leaves

Puree water, sugar, and thawed strawberries in a blender. Pour mixture into a sorbet maker and freeze until almost firm. Stir regularly. Dip out into another container with a lid. Freeze until ready to serve. Form small sorbet balls with an ice-cream scoop. Garnish with fresh strawberries and mint. Serves 12.

Strawberry Muffins

18   ounces quick oats
1   quart (4 cups) buttermilk
1   pound light brown sugar
1 1/2 cups (3 sticks) margarine, melted & cooled
6   eggs, slightly beaten

3   cups all-purpose flour
4   teaspoons baking powder
1   teaspoon salt
1 1/2 teaspoons baking soda
1   12-ounce jar strawberry preserves

Mix together oats and buttermilk in a large bowl. Sprinkle brown sugar on top and let mixture stand for one hour.

Preheat oven to 400 F. Grease mini-muffin tins. Mix melted margarine with eggs and set aside. Sift together flour, baking powder, salt, and soda. Set aside. Mix egg mixture with oat mixture. Add flour mixture and preserves . Mix together gently.

Spoon batter into muffin tins and bake 7-10 minutes. Makes 12 dozen mini-muffins. These muffins freeze well.

Cucumber Tea Sandwiches

16 slices of cracked wheat bread
1 8-ounce package cream cheese
2 tablespoons chopped fresh chives
2 tablespoons chopped fresh parsley

2 teaspoons lemon juice
1 medium cucumber, sliced thin
carrot curls

Remove crust from bread and cut into rounds. In a small bowl, combine cream cheese, chives, parsley, and lemon juice. Blend well. Spread each cutout with cream cheese mixture. Top with a cucumber slice and garnish with a carrot curl. Store in refrigerator. Makes about 32 sandwiches.

An afternoon tea for July centered around a Chocolate-Apricot Cake.

JULY AFTERNOON TEA

Maids of Honor
Raspberry Sorbet
Blueberry Muffins
Chocolate Apricot Cake
Scones with Strawberry Butter
Cucumbers with Carrots and Chives
Pineapple Kiwi Tea Sandwiches
Orange Delights
Savory Tartlets

Maids of Honor

A 16th century recipe named by Henry VIII in honor of Anne Boleyn.

2   cups all-purpose flour
1/2 cup butter, chilled
1/2 cup shortening

1 tablespoon sugar
1 egg yolk
3 teaspoons fresh lemon juice

Mix together flour and sugar. Using a pastry blender, cut butter and shortening into flour mixture until it resembles coarse crumbs. Mix egg yolk and lemon juice together. Add to flour mixture and stir until moist enough to form a ball. Do not overmix. Cover and chill 15 minutes. Grease mini-muffin tins. Pinch off enough dough to press into each muffin cup.

Filling

1/4 cup unsalted butter, room temp.
1/4 cup sugar
1   egg
1/2 cup flour

1/2 teaspoon cinnamon
1   tablespoon chopped almonds
1   teaspoon brandy
powdered sugar

Preheat oven to 350 F. Cream together butter and sugar until light and fluffy. Beat in egg and brandy. In another bowl sift together flour and cinnamon. Gently add this along with almonds to the cream mixture. Spoon about 1 teaspoon into each pastry shell. Bake for 10 to 12 minutes or until pastry is light brown and filling springs back when lightly touched. Remove from pan and place on a wire rack to cool completely. Dust with powdered sugar.

Strawberry Butter

1   cup unsalted butter, room temp.
1/4 cup strawberry preserves

1/4 cup powdered sugar

In a medium mixing bowl, beat all ingredients together until light and fluffy. Store in refrigerator.

41

Orange Delights

1   box vanilla wafers, finely crushed
1/2 cup frozen undiluted orange juice
3/4 cup sifted powdered sugar

3/4 cup flaked coconut
1/2 cup finely chopped pecans or walnuts
1/4 cup white corn syrup

Mix all ingredients together and shape into 1 inch balls. Store in a covered container in the refrigerator or freezer. When ready to serve, roll in powdered sugar. Makes 4 dozen.

Pineapple Kiwi Tea Sandwiches

1 8-ounce package cream cheese, room temp.
1/4 cup pineapple preserves
1   tablespoon mayonnaise

2 fresh kiwis, peeled and sliced thin
16 slices whole wheat bread

Remove crusts from bread and cut into rounds. In medium bowl, mix together the cream cheese, preserves, and mayonnaise. Spread evenly on top of each slice of bread. Top with a piece of kiwi. Makes 32 open-faced sandwiches.

Blueberry Muffins

18   ounces quick oats
1   quart (4 cups) buttermilk
1   pound light brown sugar
1 1/2 cups (3 sticks) margarine, melted & cooled
6   eggs, slightly beaten

3   cups all-purpose flour
4   teaspoons baking powder
1   teaspoon salt
1 1/2 teaspoons baking soda
1 1/2 cups fresh blueberries

Mix together oats and buttermilk in a large bowl. Sprinkle brown sugar on top and let mixture stand for one hour.

Preheat oven to 400 F. Grease mini-muffin tins. Mix melted margarine with eggs and set aside. Sift together flour, baking powder, salt, and soda. Set aside. Mix egg mixture with oat mixture. Add flour mixture and blueberries. Mix together gently.

Spoon batter into muffin tins and bake 7-10 minutes. Makes 12 dozen mini-muffins. These muffins freeze well.

Cucumbers with Carrots and Chives

1 large cucumber sliced into medium slices
1 3 ounce package cream cheese at room temp.
1 tablespoon chopped fresh chives
1 tablespoon chopped fresh parsley

1 teaspoon lemon juice
fresh carrot curls
pieces of leaf lettuce

Combine cream cheese, chives, parsley, and lemon juice. Blend well. Spread a small amount on top of each cucumber slice. Place cucumber on a piece of lettuce and top with a carrot curl.

Chocolate Apricot Cake
Apricots complement the flavor of this mild chocolate cake.

3   cups sifted all-purpose flour
1/2 cup unsweetened cocoa
1/2 teaspoon baking powder
1/2 teaspoon salt
1   cup unsalted butter, softened
1   tablespoon vanilla extract

1/2   cup soft shortening
3   cups sugar
5   eggs at room temperature
1 1/4 cups milk
powdered sugar

Preheat the oven to 350 F. Sift the flour with cocoa, baking powder and salt. Lightly grease and flour a 10-inch tube pan.

In a large bowl, beat together (at medium speed) butter, shortening, and sugar until light and fluffy. Add eggs, one at a time, beating well with each addition.

At low speed, beat in flour mixture, alternating with the milk. End with flour mixture. Stir in the vanilla. Turn batter into prepared pan and bake 1 hour and 10 minutes or until cake tester comes out clean. Cool in pan for 10 minutes, then turn out. Cool completely on rack. Garnish with powdered sugar and serve with apricot sauce.

Apricot Sauce

1   12-ounce jar apricot preserves
2   tablespoon lemon juice

2   tablespoons orange juice
1   tablespoon brandy (optional)

Mix all ingredients together in a small sauce pan and warm over low heat. Spoon over cake slices.

Raspberry Sorbet
The light refreshing flavor of this dish provides the perfect ending to a summer afternoon tea. We use small mint leaves from our garden as a garnish.

1 1/2 cups cold water
1/4   cup powdered sugar

2 10-ounce packages frozen raspberries in syrup
fresh raspberries and mint leaves

In a blender, puree water, powdered sugar, and raspberries. Pour through sieve to remove seeds. Pour into a sorbet maker and freeze until ready to use. Use an ice cream scoop to place servings into sherbert dishes. Garnish with fresh raspberries and mint leaves. Makes 12 servings.

An August garden tea.

AUGUST AFTERNOON TEA

Sachertorte Cookies
Lemon Glazed Cake
Waldorf Celery Boats
Raspberry Tea Sandwiches
Scones with Blackberry Preserves
Ritz Tea Sandwiches
Pineapple Sorbet
Date Nut Muffins
Savory Tartlets

Sachertorte Cookies

These elegant cookies remind you of rich chocolate desserts found in the fine restaurants of Vienna.

1 cup unsalted butter, softened
1 4 1/2-ounce package instant chocolate pudding
1 egg
2 cups flour

3   tablespoons sugar
1/2 cup apricot or cherry preserves
1/2 cup semi-sweet chocolate chips
3   tablespoons butter

Heat oven to 325 F. Mix together 1 cup butter and all the pudding mix until light and fluffy. Add egg and flour, blend well. Shape dough into 1-inch balls. Roll in sugar and place 2 inches apart on an ungreased cookie sheet. Make an indentation in the center of each cookie with the flat part of your thumb.

Bake for 15 to 18 minutes or until firm. Remove from sheets to a wire rack and cool completely. Fill each indentation with about 1/2 teaspoon preserves.

In a sauce pan, melt chocolate chips and 3 tablespoons butter and stir until smooth. Drizzle glaze over each cookie. Makes 4 dozen cookies.

Ritz Tea Sandwiches

The Ritz Hotel in London, England serves a variety of tea sandwiches at their afternoon teas. One of our favorites is a combination of cottage cheese with carrots and hazelnuts.

16 slices cracked wheat bread
1   cup small curd cottage cheese
1/2 cup grated carrot

1/4 cup chopped toasted hazelnuts
fresh parsley to garnish
salt to taste

Remove crusts from bread and cut into desired shapes with cookie cutter. Combine cottage cheese, carrot, and hazelnut in a medium bowl. Mix together well. Add a little salt if desired. Spread some of the mixture on top of each cutout. Garnish with a piece of fresh parsley. Makes 32 open-faced sandwiches.

Pineapple Sorbet

2 cups unsweetened pineapple juice
2 tablespoons cream of coconut

juice and zest of 1 lime

In a blender, mix all ingredients. Pour mixture into a sorbet maker and freeze until almost firm. Scoop out into a container with a cover. Store in freezer until ready to serve. Makes about 1 pint.

Raspberry Tea Sandwiches

16 slices white bread
1 8-ounce package cream cheese, room temp.
3 tablespoons raspberry preserves

1/2 cup fresh raspberries
fresh mint leaves

Remove crusts from bread and cut out into desired shapes with a cookie cutter. In a small mixing bowl, combine cream cheese and raspberry preserves. Spread a thin layer of the mixture on each cutout. Garnish with fresh raspberries and mint. Makes 32 open-faced sandwiches.

Waldorf Celery Boats

2 stalks fresh crisp celery
1/2 cup crumbled blue cheese
1/4 cup finely chopped toasted walnuts

1/2 cup finely chopped red delicious apple
1 teaspoon lemon juice
leaf lettuce

Cut celery into 1 1/2 inch bite-size pieces. In a medium bowl, combine blue cheese and walnuts. In a small bowl, mix the lemon juice with the chopped apple. Drain off any excess juice. Add apple to the cheese mixture. Gently mix together. Place a small amount of mixture into each piece of celery. Place each celery boat on top of a piece of leaf lettuce and serve. Serves 16.

Blackberry Preserves

Our friend and fellow gardener, Betty Hensley, brings these delicious preserves to us regularly along with warm homemade bread. This is her recipe for preserves.

2 quarts fresh blackberries
7 cups sugar

1 box fruit pectin
1/2 teaspoon butter

Crush berries and press half of the pulp through a sieve to remove some of the seeds. Measure 5 cups of crushed berries into a 6-8 quart cooking pot. Add fruit pectin and butter. Bring mixture to a full rolling boil over high heat, stirring constantly.

Quickly add sugar to fruit mixture and return to full rolling boil. Boil one minute, stirring constantly. Remove from heat. Fill canning jars quickly. Clean rims and cover with flat lids. Screw bands tightly and invert jars for 5 minutes, then turn upright. After 1 hour, check lids for sealing.

Date-Nut Muffins

18	ounces quick oats	3	cups all-purpose flour
1	quart (4 cups) buttermilk	4	teaspoons baking powder
1	pound light brown sugar	1	teaspoon salt
1 1/2	cups (3 sticks) margarine, melted & cooled	1 1/2	teaspoons baking soda
6	eggs, slightly beaten	1	cup chopped pecans
		1	cup chopped dates

Mix together oats and buttermilk in a large bowl. Sprinkle brown sugar on top and let mixture stand for one hour.

Preheat oven to 400 F. Grease mini-muffin tins. Mix melted margarine with eggs and set aside. Sift together flour, baking powder, salt, and soda. Set aside . Mix egg mixture with oat mixture. Add flour mixture, pecans, and dates. Mix together gently.

Spoon muffin batter into mini-muffin tins. Bake 7-10 minutes. Makes 12 dozen mini-muffins. These muffins freeze well.

Lemon Glazed Cake

This cake is a lemon-lover's delight. It looks beautiful sitting atop a glass cake stand. Serve it warm with a lemon glaze drizzled over each slice.

1	cup unsalted butter, softened	1/2	teaspoon salt
2	cups sugar	1	cup buttermilk
3	eggs, room temperature	3	tablespoons fresh lemon juice
3	cups all-purpose flour, sifted	2	tablespoons lemon zest
1/2	teaspoon baking soda		

Preheat oven to 325 F. Grease and flour a 10-inch tube pan. In a large bowl, cream butter and sugar until light and fluffy. Beat in eggs, one at a time.

Sift together flour, baking soda, and salt. Stir this dry mixture into egg mixture, alternating with buttermilk. Begin and end with dry ingredients. Add lemon juice and zest. Pour batter into tube pan. Bake for 1 hour and 5 minutes or until cake tester inserted into the middle comes out clean. Cool in pan for at least 15 minutes. Remove cake from pan and spread on glaze while still warm.

Lemon glaze

1/2 pound powdered sugar	1/4 cup fresh lemon juice
1/4 cup unsalted butter, room temp.	

Cream sugar and butter together. Mix in juice. Spread over warm cake.

Apple Cake with Hot Butter Sauce.

SEPTEMBER AFTERNOON TEA

Creme Fraiche Tarts
Javanese Shortbread
Curry Chicken Rolls
Tomato Basil Sandwiches
Apple Cake with Hot Butter Sauce
Cinnamon Crunch Muffins
Scones with Lemon Curd
Blueberry Sorbet
Savory Tartlets

Apple Cake with Hot Butter Sauce

1 cup unsalted butter
2 cups granulated sugar
2 eggs
2 cups thick applesauce
3 cups all-purpose flour

1 teaspoon cinnamon
1 teaspoon fresh grated nutmeg
2 teaspoons baking soda
1 teaspoon vanilla extract

Preheat oven to 325 F. Grease and flour a 10-inch tube pan. In a large mixing bowl, cream butter and sugar together until fluffy. Beat in one egg at a time. Stir in applesauce and vanilla.

In a medium bowl, sift together flour, cinnamon, nutmeg, and baking soda. Gradually add flour mixture to applesauce mixture and blend thoroughly. Pour batter evenly into tube pan. Bake for 1 hour and 10 minutes or until a cake tester comes out clean. Cool in pan for 15 minutes. Turn out on rack to cool.

Hot butter sauce

1 cup sugar
1/2 cup unsalted butter

1/2 cup heavy whipping cream
1 tablespoon bourbon (optional)

Melt butter in a small sauce pan. Add sugar, cream, and bourbon. Bring slowly to a boil. Stir until sugar is dissolved. Remove from heat. Cool slightly and serve over apple cake slices.

Tomato Basil Tea Sandwiches

16 slices white bread
32 slices Roma tomatoes
mayonnaise

mixture of dried herbs
small fresh basil leaves
salt to taste

Remove crusts from bread and cut into rounds. Mix the dried herbs, mayonnaise and salt together and spread thinly over each cut-out. Top each with a tomato slice and a small basil leaf. Makes 32 open-faced sandwiches.

Javanese Shortbread

This unusual shortbread can be found among the treats served in the tea room of the Boston Museum of Fine Arts.

1   cup unsalted butter, softened
3/4 cup sugar
1   cup flaked coconut

2   cups all-purpose flour
1/2 teaspoon almond extract
powdered sugar

Cream together butter and sugar, add coconut, flour and almond extract. Mix well. Chill dough until it is stiff. Form 2 half-dollar size rolls. Wrap in wax paper and refrigerate until firm enough to slice.

Cut into 1/4 inch slices. Bake on an ungreased cookie sheet in a 300 F oven for 20-30 minutes. Do not brown. Cool for 2 minutes before removing from sheets. Dust with powdered sugar. Makes 5 dozen shortbread cookies.

Creme Fraiche Tarts

Tart Shells

2   cups all-purpose flour
pinch of salt
1/2 cup shortening
1/2 cup butter, well chilled

4-5 tablespoons cold water
blueberries, raspberries, or strawberries
fresh mint leaves

Mix together flour and salt. With a pastry blender, cut butter and shortening into flour until mixture resembles coarse meal. Add cold water, a little at a time until mixture is moist enough to form a ball. Do not overmix. Cover and chill for 15 minutes.

Preheat oven to 350 F. On a floured surface, roll pastry out with a floured rolling pin. Grease mini-muffin tins. Cut pastry into 3-inch circles and press each circle into a muffin cup. Bake for 8-10 minutes. Cool completely. Fill with creme fraiche.

Creme fraiche

1 cup heavy cream
1 cup sour cream

1/2 cup powdered sugar

Mix the heavy cream, sour cream, and sugar together. Cover and let stand unrefrigerated for about 6 hours. Refrigerate for about 4 hours. Spoon into tart shells. Garnish with fresh fruit and mint.

Lemon Curd

3   eggs
1/2 cup fresh lemon juice

1/2 cup unsalted butter, melted
1   cup sugar

In the top part of a double boiler, beat eggs until frothy. Stir in lemon juice, sugar and melted butter. Place over simmering water. Stir constantly for 20 minutes. The mixture should become slightly thickened.

Remove from heat and spoon into a pint-sized container. Cool to room temperature, cover and refrigerate for at least two hours before serving. Keeps well for two weeks.

Cinnamon Crunch Muffins

18 ounces quick oats	3 cups all-purpose flour
1 quart (4 cups) buttermilk	4 teaspoons baking powder
1 pound light brown sugar	1 teaspoon salt
1 1/2 cups (3 sticks) margarine, melted & cooled	1 1/2 teaspoons baking soda
6 eggs, slightly beaten	

Mix together oats and buttermilk in a large bowl. Sprinkle brown sugar on top and let mixture stand for one hour.

Preheat oven to 400 F. Grease mini-muffin tins. Mix melted margarine with eggs and set aside. Sift together flour, baking powder, salt, and soda. Set aside. Mix egg mixture with oat mixture. Add flour mixture. Mix together gently.

Topping

1/2 stick unsalted butter   1/4 cup brown sugar
1/2 cup all-purpose flour   2 teaspoons cinnamon

Mix together all ingredients into a crumbly mixture. Set aside.

Spoon batter into muffin tins. Sprinkle about 1/2 teaspoon of topping over each unbaked muffin. Bake 7-10 minutes. Makes 12 dozen mini-muffins. These muffins freeze well.

Curry Chicken Rolls

6 ounces cream cheese, room temp.	3 cups finely chopped cooked chicken
2 tablespoons orange marmalade	3 tablespoons minced onion
2 teaspoons curry powder	3 tablespoons minced celery
1/4 teaspoon pepper	1 cup finely chopped almonds, toasted
1/4 teaspoon salt	

In a mixing bowl, combine first five ingredients. Beat until smooth. Stir in the chicken, onion, and celery. Shape into 1-inch balls and roll in almonds. Chill for two days or freeze up to one month. Makes 3 1/2 dozen.

Blueberry Sorbet

1 15-ounce can blueberries   1/4 cup sugar
1/2 cup water

Drain syrup from blueberries. Add syrup to sugar and water. Heat just until the sugar dissolves. Add blueberries and chill thoroughly.

Pour mixture into a sorbet maker and freeze until almost firm. Turn frequently. Spoon into a container with a cover and freeze until ready to serve. Garnish each scoop with fresh mint or fresh blueberries.

A country tea.

OCTOBER AFTERNOON TEA

Pumpkin Cake
Orange Galettes
Olive Nut Sandwiches
Scones with Apricot Butter
Raspberry Lemon Muffins
Jack-o-lantern Shortbread
Country Ham Biscuits
Savory Tartlets
Orange Sorbet

Pumpkin Cake with Cream

3	cups granulated sugar	1/4	teaspoon salt
1	cup shortening	1	teaspoon soda
3	eggs, beaten	1	teaspoon cinnamon
2	cups pumpkin, cooked & pureed	1	teaspoon nutmeg
1	teaspoon vanilla	1	teaspoon allspice
3	cups all-purpose flour	1	teaspoon ginger
1/2	teaspoon baking powder		fresh unsweetened whipped cream
1	teaspoon cloves		

Preheat oven to 350 F. Grease and flour a 10-inch tube pan. Cream together shortening and sugar. Add eggs, pumpkin, and vanilla. Sift dry ingredients together and add to creamed mixture. Pour mixture into tube pan and smooth top. Bake for 1 hour and 15 minutes or until cake tester comes out clean. Serve with fresh unsweetened whipped cream.

Jack-o-lantern Shortbread

2	cups unsalted butter, room temp.	4	cups all-purpose flour
1	cup sugar	1	cup finely-chopped almonds
1	teaspoon almond extract		red and yellow food coloring

In a large mixing bowl, beat butter and sugar together until fluffy. Add almond extract and a dash of salt. Beat well. Add flour until well-mixed.

Blend in a few drops of yellow and red food color until the desired orange color is achieved. Stir in almonds.

On a floured surface, roll out dough to 1/4 inch thickness. Cut out with a jack-o-lantern cookie cutter. Place cookies on an ungreased cookie sheet. Bake in a 325 F oven about 20 minutes. Do not brown. Cool on a wire rack.

Olive Nut Tea Sandwiches

16 slices cracked wheat bread
1 8-ounce package cream cheese, room temp.
1/4 cup chopped walnuts

1/4 cup chopped olives
1 tablespoon mayonnaise
sliced olives and parsley for garnish

Remove crusts from bread and cut into desired shapes. Mix together the cream cheese, walnuts, chopped olives and mayonnaise. Spread evenly over each cut-out. Garnish with an olive slice and a piece of parsley. Makes 32 open-faced sandwiches.

Orange Galettes
These small tarts filled with orange sauce add a wonderful color to any Fall occasion.

Tart Shells

2 cups all-purpose flour
pinch of salt
1/2 cup butter, chilled

4-5 tablespoons cold water
1/2 cup shortening

Mix together flour and salt. With a pastry blender, cut the butter and shortening into flour until mixture resembles coarse meal. Add cold water, a little at a time, until the mixture is moist enough to form a ball. Do not overmix. Cover and chill for 15 minutes.

Preheat oven to 350 F. On a floured surface, roll pastry out with a floured rolling pin. Grease mini-muffin tins. Cut pastry into 3-inch circles and press each circle into a mini-muffin cup. Bake for 8-10 minutes. Cool completely.

Filling

3/4 cup sugar
2 1/2 tablespoons cornstarch
1/8 teaspoon salt
1/2 cup fresh orange juice
1/2 cup water
3 tablespoons orange zest

2 tablespoons lemon juice
2 tablespoons butter
1 medium can mandarin oranges
1 6 ounce bag semi-sweet chocolate morsels
   (melted)

In a small sauce pan, combine sugar, cornstarch, and salt. Gradually stir in orange juice and 1/2 cup water over medium heat. Bring mixture to boiling and continue for 1 minute. Remove from heat. Stir in orange zest, lemon juice, and butter. Cool.

Fill each shell with 1 tablespoon of mixture, top with 1 orange section and drizzle chocolate over the top. Makes about 48 tarts.

Orange Sorbet

2 cups fresh orange juice, strained
1/4 cup powdered sugar

1 tablespoon orange zest

Squeeze enough oranges to make two cups of juice. Grate 1 tablespoon zest. In a blender, blend all ingredients until smooth and pour into a sorbet maker. Freeze until almost firm. Stir often. Spoon into a container. Cover and freeze until ready to serve. Garnish with orange slices.

Country Ham Biscuits

Central Kentucky is known for its world-famous country ham. These small ham biscuits are a perfect complement to the sweet items on our fall menu.

1/2 pound thinly sliced country ham
2 cups flour .
4 teaspoons baking powder
1/2 teaspoon baking soda

1/2 teaspoon salt
1/4 cup shortening
1 cup buttermilk

Combine flour, baking powder, soda, and salt. With a pastry blender, cut in the shortening until mixture resembles cornmeal. Pour in buttermilk, stirring just until dough holds together.

Knead lightly 5 or 6 times on a floured surface. Roll out to 1/2 inch thickness and cut out with a 2-inch biscuit cutter. Place on an ungreased cookie sheet and bake at 450 F for 10 minutes. Remove from pan and place on a wire rack. Stuff with country ham and serve warm or cold.

Raspberry Lemon Muffins

18 ounces quick oats
1   quart (4 cups) buttermilk
1   pound light brown sugar
1 1/2 cups (3 sticks) margarine, melted & cooled
6   eggs, slightly beaten

3   cups all-purpose flour
4   teaspoons baking powder
1   teaspoon salt
1 1/2 teaspoons baking soda
1   pint fresh raspberries
zest of 1 lemon

Mix together oats and buttermilk in a large bowl. Sprinkle brown sugar on top and let mixture stand for one hour.

Preheat oven to 400 F. Grease mini-muffin tins. Mix melted margarine with the eggs and set aside. Sift together flour, baking powder, salt, and soda. Set aside . Mix egg mixture with oat mixture. Add flour mixture, raspberries, and zest. Mix together gently.

Spoon batter into muffin tins and bake 7-10 minutes. Makes 12 dozen mini- muffins. These muffins freeze well.

Apricot Butter

Your tea guests or breakfast guests will be surprised to find the wonderful taste of apricots blended with their butter. It's a special treat that you can always keep handy in your refrigerator.

1 cup unsalted butter, room temperature   1/4 cup powdered sugar
1/4 cup apricot preserves

In a medium bowl, beat all ingredients together until light and fluffy. Store in refrigerator until ready to serve with scones or muffins.

55

Twilight tea featuring Edinburgh Fog.

NOVEMBER AFTERNOON TEA

Edinburgh Fog
Lady Baltimore Tarts
Scones with Citrus Curd
Chutney Pear Sandwiches
Ham and Pineapple Sandwiches
Pumpkin Ginger Muffins
Cheddar Cheese Wafers
Brownie Tea Cakes
Savory Tartlets

Edinburgh Fog

This adaptation of a very old Scottish recipe is a favorite at the inn. It was originally conceived to make use of leftover scones in the Scottish household. We like to use crumbled pound cake in place of scones.

1 cup heavy whipping cream
2 tablespoons powdered sugar
1 teaspoon vanilla extract

1/2 cup crumbled pound cake
1/2 cup blanched almonds, chopped

Beat cream to a stiff froth with sugar and vanilla. Mix thoroughly with crumbled cake and almonds. Chill well and serve in dessert goblets with fruit sauce on top.

Fruit sauce
3/4 cup fresh orange juice
2 tablespoons sugar
1 tablespoon cornstarch
1/4 cup strawberries

1/4 cup grapes
1/4 cup mandarin oranges, drained
1/4 cup raspberries
1 tablespoon lemon juice

Combine sugar and cornstarch in a small saucepan. Gradually add orange juice and bring to a boil. Lower heat and add the remaining ingredients. Heat thoroughly but do not boil. Remove from heat. Chill. Spoon over individual servings of Edinburgh Fog.

Cheddar Cheese Wafers

2 cups sharp cheddar cheese, shredded
2 cups self-rising flour
2 cups crispy rice cereal

2 sticks butter, softened
1 teaspoon salt
1/2 teaspoon red pepper

Mix all ingredients by hand in a large bowl. Roll into small balls. Place on an ungreased cookie sheet and flatten each with a fork. Bake at 350 F for ten minutes. Makes 3 dozen.

Lady Baltimore Tarts

These tarts are an adaptation of the famous cake served in Charleston's Lady Baltimore Tea Room.

3 eggs, well beaten	1/2 cup chopped red candied cherries
1 1/2 cups firmly packed brown sugar	1 teaspoon vanilla extract
1/2 cup light corn syrup	1/2 teaspoon almond extract
1 1/2 cups chopped pecan or walnuts	16 (3 inch) unbaked commercial tart shells
1 cup flaked coconut	

Preheat oven to 300 F. Combine first 3 ingredients until well-blended. Stir in the nuts, coconut, chopped cherries, and extracts.

Place unbaked tart shells on an ungreased cookie sheet. Spoon 1/4 cup of mixture into each tart shell. Bake for 40 minutes or until set. Remove from oven and cool. Serves 16.

Brownie Tea Cakes

3/4 cup butter	1 cup all-purpose flour
2 squares semi-sweet chocolate	2 tablespoons cocoa
1 square unsweetened chocolate	1/8 teaspoon salt
1 3/4 cups sugar	1 cup walnuts, toasted and chopped
4 eggs	powdered sugar
1 teaspoon vanilla extract	

Preheat oven to 350 F. Melt butter and chocolate over low heat. Remove from heat and stir in sugar. Add eggs, one at a time, stirring well with each addition. Add vanilla.

Combine flour, cocoa, and salt. Add this to the chocolate mixture. Stir with a wire whisk until smooth. Stir in chopped walnuts.

Spoon batter into paper-lined mini-muffin pans, filling 3/4 full. Bake at 350 F for 12 to 15 minutes. Cool and dust with powdered sugar. Makes 32 brownie cakes.

Pumpkin Ginger Muffins

2 cups all-purpose flour	1/2 teaspoon cloves
1 cup brown sugar, packed	1 teaspoon crystallized ginger
1 teaspoon baking powder	1/2 teaspoon grated nutmeg
1/2 teaspoon baking soda	1/2 cup melted unsalted butter, cooled
1/2 teaspoon salt	1/4 cup apple juice
1/2 teaspoon cinnamon	2 eggs
1 teaspoon ground ginger	1 cup pumpkin

Preheat oven to 400 F. Grease and set aside mini-muffin tins.

In a large bowl, combine the flour, sugar, baking powder, soda, salt, and spices. In a separate bowl, combine melted butter, juice, eggs, and pumpkin. Add wet mixture to dry mixture, stirring until well-moistened. Spoon batter into the tins and bake for 7-10 minutes. Makes about 6 dozen muffins.

Chutney Pear Tea Sandwiches

16 slices dark rye bread
1 8-ounce package cream cheese, room temp.
1/4 cup peach or mango chutney, finely chopped

1 pear, unpeeled and thinly sliced
fresh parsley

Remove crust from bread and cut into rounds. Mix the cream cheese and chutney together. Spread each cut-out with the cream cheese mixture. Brush pear slices lightly with lemon juice and place on top of each round. Garnish with fresh parsley. Makes 32 open-faced sandwiches.

Ham and Pineapple Tea Sandwiches

16 slices whole wheat bread
1/4 pound lean cooked ham, chopped finely
in a food processor
1 tablespoon mayonnaise

1/2 tablespoon honey mustard
32 tiny wedges of fresh pineapple
fresh cilantro

Remove crust from bread and cut out into desired shapes. Mix ham, mayonnaise, and mustard together. Spread mixture over each bread cutout. Top with fresh pineapple and cilantro. Makes 32 sandwiches.

Citrus Curd

3 eggs
1/4 cup fresh orange juice
1/4 cup fresh lime juice

2 tablespoons fresh lemon juice
1/2 cup unsalted butter, melted
1 cup sugar

In the top of a double boiler, beat the eggs until frothy. In a separate bowl, combine the juices. Add all the ingredients to eggs and place over simmering water. Stir constantly for 20 minutes. The mixture should become slightly thickened. Remove from heat and spoon into a pint-sized container. Cool to room temperature, cover, and refrigerate for at least two hours before serving. Keeps well for two weeks.

Christmas tea with Austrian Linzer Torte.

DECEMBER AFTERNOON TEA

Austrian Linzer Torte
Cranberry Orange Muffins
Bread Pudding with Bourbon Sauce
Roast Beef Sandwiches with Horseradish
Scones with Cranberry Curd
Christmas Tree Sandwiches
Mocha Filled Cream Puffs
Cherry Cheese Tarts
Savory Tartlets

Austrian Linzer Torte

This classic holiday torte looks beautiful decorated with holly leaves - an almond lover's delight!

1   cup butter, chilled and sliced
2 1/4 cups sifted all-purpose flour
1   cup sugar
1 1/4 cups almonds (chopped fine in food processor)
juice of 1/2 lemon
1/4 teaspoon cinnamon
1/4 teaspoon cloves
1/4 teaspoon nutmeg
1   teaspoon almond extract
4   egg yolks
1   egg well-beaten
1   cup raspberry preserves
sliced almonds

With a pastry blender, cut butter into flour. Add sugar, almonds, lemon juice, spices, and egg yolks. Knead with your hands until well-mixed. Turn onto a floured surface and knead until a smooth ball forms. Wrap in plastic and chill for 1 hour.

On the bottom of an ungreased 10-inch springform pan, place 1/2 the dough and pat out evenly. Make a 1/2 -inch rope of dough and place around the edge of the first layer of dough. Spread the raspberry preserves evenly over the dough. Use remaining dough to make a lattice over the preserves. Brush lattice with beaten egg. Place sliced almonds around the outer edge atop the rope of dough. Bake at 400 F for 10 minutes, then lower to 325 F and bake for 30 minutes. Cool in pan. Remove pan rim and slice into small servings.

Christmas Tree Tea Sandwiches

2 onions
2 seeded cucumbers
2 carrots
1 tablespoon gelatin
2   tablespoons hot water
1 1/2 cups mayonnaise
1   teaspoon salt
bread cut into 32 small Christmas trees

Grate onions, cucumber, and carrots. Dissolve gelatin in hot water, cool. Mix mayonnaise with vegetables. Add salt and gelatin, stirring constantly. Refrigerate for 8 hours. Spread mixture over bread pieces and garnish with a small piece of parsley at the top to resemble a star.

Cranberry Curd

My longtime friend and fellow antique-lover, Margaret Lane, is always finding unusual recipes. She shares this rendition of a classic English recipe with a Colonial flavor.

4 cups frozen cranberries, thawed	1/2 cup unsalted butter
1/2 cup fresh orange juice	2 tablespoons Grand Marnier
1 cup sugar	1 tablespoon grated orange zest
4-6 large egg yolks	

Place berries, orange juice, and sugar in a sauce pan. Cook over medium heat until berries are very soft. Stir frequently. Process mixture through a sieve. Discard skins and seeds. Taste puree for sweetness. You may need to add more sugar. Whisk in egg yolks (6 for a richer puree) and cook over low heat. Stir constantly until mixture is very thick. Remove from heat and gradually add pieces of butter until all are melted. Stir in Grand Marnier and zest. Cool and refrigerate before serving with scones.

Cherry Cheese Tarts

Crust

1 1/4 cups graham cracker crumbs	Dash of cinnamon and nutmeg
1/2 stick unsalted butter	48 mini-cupcake liners

Place cupcake liners in mini-muffin tins. Mix all of ingredients and press 1 teaspoon of the mixture into each liner.

Filling

1 pound cream cheese	1/2 cup sugar
2 eggs	1 small can cherry pie filling
1/2 teaspoon vanilla	

Beat all ingredients (excluding cherries) together until smooth. Fill the cupcake papers 3/4 full. Bake 10 minutes at 375 F. Cool and place one cherry on top of each tart. Refrigerate until ready to serve.

Cranberry Orange Muffins

18 ounces quick oats	3 cups all-purpose flour
1 quart (4 cups) buttermilk	4 teaspoons baking powder
1 pound light brown sugar	1 teaspoon salt
1 1/2 cups (3 sticks) margarine, melted & cooled	1 1/2 teaspoons baking soda
6 eggs, slightly beaten	1 1/2 cups chopped fresh cranberries
3 tablespoons orange zest	

Mix together oats and buttermilk in a large bowl. Sprinkle brown sugar on top and let mixture stand for one hour.

Preheat oven to 400 F. Grease mini-muffin tins. Mix melted margarine with eggs and set aside. Sift together flour, baking powder, salt, and soda. Set aside. Mix egg mixture with oat mixture. Add flour mixture, zest, and cranberries. Mix together gently.

Spoon into mini-muffin tins and bake for 7-10 minutes. Makes 12 dozen.

Mocha-filled Cream Puffs

Cream puffs
1/2 cup water
1/4 cup butter

1/2 cup unsifted all-purpose flour
2 large eggs
1/8 teaspoon salt

In a sauce pan, combine water, butter, and salt. Bring to a boil. Remove from heat. Beat in flour with a spoon. Return to low heat and beat mixture until a ball forms (2 minutes). Remove from heat. Add 1 egg and beat with an electric mixer until blended. Add other egg and beat until dough is shiny. Drop teaspoons of the mixture, 2 inches apart, onto an ungreased cookie sheet. Bake 20 minutes at 400 F. Cool on a rack.

Cream filling
1 1/2 cups heavy cream
1/2 cup powdered sugar
1/4 cup cocoa

2 teaspoons instant coffee
1 teaspoon vanilla

In a large mixing bowl, combine all ingredients and mix until stiff. Assemble the puffs by cutting off top of each one. Remove any soft dough from inside. Fill with mocha filling and replace the top. Sprinkle with powdered sugar and serve. Make 36 puffs.

Roast Beef Sandwiches with Horseradish

16 slices pumpernickel bread
3 tablespoons mayonnaise
1 1/2 tablespoons prepared horseradish
fresh parsley

8 ounces thinly sliced roast beef
sliced radishes
salt and pepper to taste

Remove crusts from bread and cut into triangles. Combine mayonnaise and horseradish. Place a small slice of roast beef on each slice of bread. (Fold the roast beef to conform to the size of the bread.) Season with salt and pepper. Spoon a little horseradish sauce over beef. Place another triangle of bread on top. Garnish with a radish slice and parsley sprig. Makes 16 sandwiches.

Bread Pudding with Bourbon Sauce

Elmwood Inn is only an hour's drive from most of Kentucky's famous bourbon distilleries.

6 ounces day-old bread with crust
2 cups milk
2 eggs
1 cup sugar

1/2 cup butter, melted
4 tablespoons vanilla
1 tablespoon melted butter

Preheat oven to 350 F. Place the bread into a large mixing bowl. Add milk and let sit until milk is absorbed. In a separate bowl, beat the eggs. Add sugar, butter, and vanilla. Mix well. Add this mixture to bread and milk.. Coat a 2-quart glass baking dish with 1 tablespoon of melted butter. Pour bread mixture into baking dish. Bake at 350 F for 45 minutes to 1 hour. Pudding should be firm and light golden brown. Spoon out into separate dessert dishes and serve with bourbon sauce.

Bourbon sauce
1 cup sugar
1/2 cup unsalted butter

1/2 cup heavy cream
1 tablespoon bourbon

Melt butter in a small sauce pan. Add sugar and cream. Bring slowly to a boil. Add bourbon. Turn heat to low and cook for about 1 minute. Remove from heat. Serve hot over bread pudding.

INDEX